DEVI2DIVA

Disclaimer

This publication is protected under the International Copyright Order, 1999 and all other applicable international, state and local laws, and all rights are reserved, including resale rights.

Please note that much of this publication is based on personal experience and anecdotal evidence. Although the author and publisher have made every reasonable attempt to achieve complete accuracy of the content in this Guide, they assume no responsibility for errors or omissions.

Also, you should use this information as you see fit, and at your own risk. Your particular situation may not be exactly suited to the examples illustrated here; and you are advised to adjust your use of the information and recommendations accordingly.

Any trademarks, service marks, product names or named features are assumed to be the property of their respective owners, and are used only for reference. There is no implied endorsement if we use one of these terms, unless specifically indicated.

Finally, use your head. Nothing in this book is intended to replace common sense, legal, medical or other professional advice.

DEVI 2 DIVA

Authored by

PRIYA FLORENCE SHAH

Penman Books

Office No. 303, Kumar House Building,
D Block, Central Market, Opp PVR Cinema,
Prashant Vihar, Delhi 110085, India
Website: www.penmanbooks.com
Email: publish@penmanbooks.com

First Published by Penman Books 2019
Copyright © Priya Florence Shah 2019
All Rights Reserved.

Title: Devi2Diva
ISBN: 978-93-89024-01-2

Dedication

This book is dedicated to
my parents, Merle and Gerry de Souza,
who first taught me about life and love.

Acknowledgment

It is from our friends, family and teachers that we learn about ourselves and how to navigate the rocky road of relationships on this planet.

I would like to acknowledge my child, Elijah Shah, who has taught me so much about being a mom and about how much I have yet to learn.

I am grateful to my partner, Arun Chitnis, for being a sounding board for my ideas and rants since 2008.

I would like to acknowledge my teachers, Richard Carlson, Pema Chodron, Margaret Paul, and Esther Hicks, whose books and teachings have opened up my mind to new ways of thinking and being.

Foreword

Women may be 50% of the population, but in our world, 80% of history, religion, science and art has been written by men and about men. It is not good or bad – it is just the way it has been.

We have not had our voice. As a consequence, we have grown up feeling our duty is to be there for the men. So whenever we do things for ourselves, we often feel like we do a lot of things wrong, we hold onto guilt, and we question ourselves.

Why? Because we are measuring ourselves by ideals set by men. We are the by-product of their life.

As a child, I always felt like a misfit in the chauvinistic, misogynistic English world of the seventies. With immigrant parents who were fighting hard to keep an Indian culture at home, and a British world fighting hard to keep their culture outside, it was confusing.

Everything I did was not right or good enough. So I tried hard to be better than and excel. In some ways it worked – I sold my first company when I was 27 and went on to build others across continents.

I was recognised by governments, even Her Majesty the Queen of England with an OBE (equivalent of a Padmashree) but I still never felt good enough. I always felt like an impostor – that people would find out I am fraud underneath it all. And I was miserable, but showed a happy face to the outside world.

Then something happened. One evening a woman confided in me that she felt like an outsider – that she didn't belong. She had given her life to her parents, her husband, her inlaws and her children, that she had forgotten who she was underneath.

This resonated so much! And then more I talked to women, the more I saw how much they were grappling under the surface with life being about the person others wanted them to be, but forgetting who THEY were inside.

And then I started reading on the web – I came across Naaree.com. My heart started to sing because finally here was a woman talking about all the things that I felt but could not put words to. That woman was Priya Florence Shah.

She was articulating the words that were going around my head and coming up with practical reasons about why it was nonsense. Why I could be who I was inside. Advice on working from home, building a career, improving myself, dealing with difficult relationships and much more.

By chance we met at an event and we just hugged each other. She had also read about me, my success and my struggles. She could see the work I was doing for women and entrepreneurship and was so supportive.

When I heard her story, her struggles and her life, I was in awe. When she asked me to write this foreword I was beyond honoured because she is a soul-sister in every sense of the word.

Women are waking up. And realising life does not have to be this way. That maybe, just maybe, the world has got it wrong. I cannot overstate how important it is going to be for ALL women EVERYWHERE, to read "From Devi to Diva" and reclaim their life.

Priya Florence Shah has written something so valuable – there is a jewel in every page.

Breathe. Enjoy this book and allow yourself to find the real you – the one that has been hidden under those layers of responsibility and duty. Bring out your inner Diva by diving into this book.

Sometimes destruction comes before creation and you will have to destroy certain traits in yourself in order to create something new. Priya teaches you to see how pleasing others and/or blaming others (which we as women do far too much!) are just ways of not taking responsibility for yourself.

She then shows you how to build inner security so that you don't need to rely on anyone, that you can do it yourself. That you are responsible for your happiness and that when you are content, those around you will be too.

Encourage others to read it so they can find the light that they so desperately seek in this dark world.

For when they do this, we will have a battalion of empowered women who can say to their daughters, "This is our place. Right here. And this is our voice. And you are the light, not the shadow anymore."

Vandana Saxena Poria FCA OBE

Preface

In India, "Devi" means Goddess. Unfortunately, Indian women are expected – by society, family and peers - to express the best qualities of the Goddess, while being treated like lesser beings.

A "Diva", on the other hand, is a woman who is badass - unafraid of expressing herself and choosing her own life path - who doesn't look to other people or to society for approval.

If you're weary from the weight of other people's expectations and worn-out from conforming to everyone else's image of what the "perfect Indian woman" should be, this message is for you.

Are you ready to transform into a Diva - a woman who is **proud to be herself**, who is a fierce and fearless force for change?

A Diva is a woman who has come into her own power, who can change her life - and the lives of everyone around her - with clarity and compassion.

This book will transform you from a Devi, a woman who conforms to society's expectations – to a Diva, someone who chooses to live life by her own values and ideals.

Who chooses what is right for her over what is expected of her.

In this course, you'll learn how to throw off the shackles of your own **limiting beliefs**, rewrite your life story and design your destiny.

You'll learn to **stop measuring yourself by other people's expectations** and accept yourself fully and completely for who you are and choose to be.

You'll learn to tune in to the unlimited potential you have – to create and contribute.

You'll learn to become fierce and fearless with a caring community of women who support you in **becoming a powerful force for change**.

Are you ready to transform yourself from Devi 2 Diva?

Contents

CHAPTER
One

Seeta and Geeta

Most Indian women of my era will remember an old Hindi movie called '*Seeta Aur Geeta*', starring Hema Malini in a double role as a pair of twins with very different personalities - one who is literally a *Devi* (who caters to everyone else's needs), and the other a *Diva*.

To many Indian women of that time, the roles were metaphors for the women who reside inside all of us, *Devi* and *Diva*. These are the roles we enact in different contexts of our lives; they dictate the behaviors that rule our relationships with the significant people in our life:

The meek and ever-suffering Seeta - pandering to husband, in-laws and families.

The feisty Geeta - the woman who knows how she wants to be treated and demands respect.

While these two are extremes, our true selves lie somewhere in between. We are often confused about the right way to act or assert ourselves, and give in resentfully when we should not and or assert ourselves aggressively when it is unnecessary.

Now, who am I to offer advice on this? Well, let me tell you my story.

I lost the love of my life - my husband of 12 years and companion of 18 - to a sudden, massive heart attack in 2005.

My child was just 6 at the time. Though I had started building a business because of financial problems we suffered during a downturn, I depended on my husband for everything related to my life – my finances, my social life… everything.

When he passed away, I was left with the considerable task of managing as a widow in a rather unsupportive society. For those not in the know, Indian society is notorious for its condescending attitude towards widows, and for treating them with little more than pity and disdain.

In my journey to regain my shattered self-confidence and rebuild my life, I attracted people and situations that told me I desperately needed to build stronger boundaries and set limits on what I was willing to tolerate in my life.

So I get remarried and then I got divorced after 8 years, having realized that I don't really care for the rules of society anyway and that marriage is not an empowering way of living for a woman like me who loves her freedom and independence.

I expand on this in the chapter on the "Brules" (or bullshit rules) that I discarded to become a much happier person.

The biggest lesson in my life, though, was the realization that people treat you the way you allow yourself to be treated, and that your relationships with others are a reflection of the relationship you have with yourself.

THE RELATIONSHIP YOU HAVE WITH YOURSELF IS THE MOST IMPORTANT RELATIONSHIP IN YOUR LIFE.

In the following chapters, I will help you see the role you play in creating your life the way it is now. I will offer actionable steps to turn things around, so that you are no longer left tired, drained and frustrated from giving to the endless demands of the people in your life.

I hope that, with the help of the lessons I have learned over years of trial by fire, I can help you make your own journey from *Devi* to *Diva*.

CHAPTER
Two

Stopping The Blame Game

If you're a spiritual person (and I hope you are, because this book is based in spirituality), you may have read or heard that the reason we attract difficult people in our lives is because we have emotions or issues that we need to heal in ourselves.

The people we attract into our lives are our teachers. They are the ones who will trigger the very emotions that we need to heal.

Now, when you realize that the people in your life are there because YOU attracted them in the first place, it can be a very empowering feeling.

Because when you have realized and accepted this, you can take responsibility for healing the issues and emotions that these people are bringing up for you.

You cannot change what you refuse to accept. You can only change how you react to people when you accept that you're **<u>ALLOWING</u>** them to trigger you.

So, now instead of **blaming your mother-in-law** for laying her guilt trip on you, you can ask yourself, why am I letting her make me feel guilty?

And you can thank her (inwardly, of course) for helping you **<u>REALIZE</u>** that you need to heal the issue that is making you feel guilty in the first place.

And before you blame your husband's behavior for stirring up feelings of rejection or abandonment, ask yourself why you feel that way in the first place.

Most likely it was a **feeling of rejection or abandonment** you felt in your childhood and that you now need to heal in yourself.

Your emotional issues, or the things that trigger you, are like a computer program that runs every time a button is pressed.

When you become aware of your programming, and rewrite the code, what other people say or do will no longer trigger you or press your buttons, and you won't feel the need to react to them as you did before.

The minute you realize where that emotion came from, your reactions will start to shift and you will have the freedom, and more importantly, the **CHOICE** to respond calmly and assertively instead of reacting from hurt or anger.

It is our childhood wounds and conditioning that keep us tied to old ways of behaving that no longer serve us in our relationships.

One of my favourite teachers, bestselling author and American Buddhist nun, Pema Chödrön, calls this *shenpa*, the Tibetan word for attachment, which is translated as "something that hooks us".

When you stop the cycle of reacting from the "wounded child" or from your conditioning, you'll break the karmic cycle that you and the other people in your life are playing out with each other.

When the lesson is finally learned, you can let go of the pain it was creating in your life and you can now choose to **<u>respond in a calm and compassionate manner</u>**.

Seeing you respond in this manner will make others take you seriously and they, in turn, will give you the respect you deserve.

It is very freeing to realize that something or someone no longer triggers you in the old ways. It feels great when you can choose the way you respond rather than let yourself react from old patterns and conditioning.

Your relationships will transform when you give up blame and choose to take responsibility for responding from a position of strength.

And then, as a wise man called Lao Tzu, said, you will be able to "Respond intelligently even to unintelligent treatment."

CHAPTER
Three

The Disease to Please

*"Care about what other people think and
you will always be their prisoner."*

—*Lao Tzu*

The disease to please is very common, especially among women and even more so among those who suffer from low self-worth and low self-esteem.

Now, the need for acceptance or belonging is very normal and very human. In fact it's one of the basic human needs, listed on Maslow's Hierarchy of Needs.

But what I have learned in my life is that accepting and being accepted by other people has its roots or origins in one's acceptance of oneself.

The need to please everyone (or be a 'people pleaser') stems from a lack of self-acceptance. This lack is what makes us try to get what we need from other people instead of giving it to ourselves.

But when you spend your life trying to please other people – your husband, your mother-in-law, your children - you are essentially giving away your power to them and making them responsible for your happiness.

When you act like a 'people-pleaser', you're giving up your own needs, ignoring your inner voice and giving up your self-respect and dignity in order to make others happy.

And in our efforts to keep everyone else happy, we end up doing too much for them and catering to everyone's needs but our own.

In doing this, you're not doing anyone a favor, believe me. Instead, you're inviting people to treat you with disrespect and to exploit you. Ask yourself, are you happy being a people pleaser? Chances are that you're not.

Your unhappiness stems not from the fact that others are taking you for granted or treating you badly, but because _in working to gain their approval, you are treating YOURSELF badly_.

And the more you do that, the more you will continue to feel unappreciated, and the stronger your feelings of resentment will become, until you can no longer ignore them.

When you do things to get approval from others and don't get the approval you seek, you'll end up resentful, you'll burn out physically and emotionally and you'll collapse from exhaustion or depression.

It's not easy to give up approval-seeking behavior when your self-acceptance and self-esteem are practically non-existent.

The cure for this is to focus on building your sense of self-esteem and realizing that you are worthy of love and acceptance just for being you.

Your sense of self-acceptance will then become so strong that even another person's disapproval will not shake the belief that you deserve love and affection, for no other reason than the fact that you exist.

Pay close attention to your motives when you offer to do something for someone else. Are you doing it without any expectation of reciprocation or because you expect something (love, affection or acceptance) in return?

Are you acting from a place of fullness and love, or from a place of lack and wanting? If you've made people-pleasing and taking care of others a habit, it will be hard to change unless you remain ever vigilant of your actions and motives.

You can get out of people-pleasing mode by starting to allow your family and friends to do things for themselves.

From folding their own clothes and putting them away to helping out in the kitchen, get your family members to do more chores for themselves.

You are not doing your kids and husband a favor by doing everything for them. Instead you are making them dependent on you, and for the wrong reasons. So, allow them to take over their own chores and start taking care of yourself for a change.

It will be hard at first, because caretaking is a habit that is hard to break, and it feels so right to keep doing it because society tells you that self-sacrifice is a positive trait. Believe me it's not.

But you will grow your self-esteem and self-worth when you start doing good things for yourself.

Start practicing extreme self-care and stop doing everything for others, especially when you realize that you are doing it for unhealthy reasons.

When you **take loving action on your own behalf**, you will have more faith in your ability to do what is right for yourself and your sense of self-worth will increase.

Take small actions everyday to nurture yourself. Set aside some time every day to pursue your own hobbies and passions or do the things that nurture you.

Building a strong mind that supports you is very much like building a bikini body. You can't expect it to happen overnight. You only get there with practice and dedication.

So, cultivate positive self-talk and do not be critical or impatient with with yourself. Realise that changing your beliefs can take time and effort.

One healing modality that I have personally found to be very effective in installing new empowering beliefs with very little effort is Hypnosis.

You can use hypnosis to reprogram a false belief in as little as 30 to 60 days of regularly listening to the right hypnosis audio.

Energy work is also a very effective way to get rid of old beliefs and programs "stuck" in our energy body. You'll find a number of programs in the online course that will help you work on your energy body and limiting beliefs.

CHAPTER
Four

Give Up The Guilt

If you've ever travelled by air, you will remember the stewardesses' instructions to put on your own oxygen mask first before helping others with theirs.

If at a critical moment, a pang of guilt prevented you from doing what you need to in order to survive, you would end up harming not only yourself but also your loved ones.

Now, Indian women have been so conditioned to believe that they are supposed to do everything at home, from cooking to cleaning up and managing everyone's needs, that not being able to do it, for whatever reason, fills us with guilt and self-judgment.

In her book, *Chup: Breaking the Silence About India's Women*, Deepa Narayan writes about the culture that devalues women and notes how Indian women are trained to habitually delete themselves, how loving parents are still training girls not to exist.

It all contributes to a lack of power or a lack of a sense of self, she notes. These messages from society, your parents and family may be why you feel guilty when you want to do something for yourself.

This guilt is something that we need to discard, so we can reclaim our power. **If thinking of carving out space**

and time for yourself makes you feel guilty, remind yourself that guilt is a wasted emotion.

It serves no one and it actually harms your ability to take care of your own needs. If you feel like you're juggling too many things without any help from your family, perhaps it's time you dropped a ball or two.

And by this I mean - STOP doing so much for others. STOP picking up after everyone else. STOP putting away your husband's and children's plates when they are perfectly capable of doing it themselves.

Tell them politely and firmly that from now onward, they must learn to do their own chores as you have enough to do. If the dirty dishes have to lie on the table for a few hours or even a day till they get the message, never mind.

Resist the urge to clean up after them, because when you are training your family to support you, consistency is the key. By giving in and cleaning up yourself, you only perpetuate a habit that you are trying to change.

Sure, things will get unpleasant for a while. The house will get messy and you will face some resistance and dissatisfaction. But **don't give in to the guilt trips** they lay on you.

When they see that you are firm in your resolve and will not back down, they will learn to adjust and start helping out more.

Now, this advice will probably not work for you if you're facing an abusive domestic situation. If that is the case, I recommend you consult a counsellor or legal expert.

Assuming that your family is caring and has just been spoiled by your self-sacrificing behaviors, my advice is to **stop doing too much for them**.

Be selfish (at least, some of the time) and learn to give priority your own needs first. If you are not selfish enough to ensure your own happiness, you are of no use to anyone else.

You can only do what is best for others when you care for them from a position of strength. If they act too demanding, **learn to say "No" kindly and mean it**.

Guilt and Parenting

As a parent, it's not easy to live guilt-free (ask me, I know!).

We're always haunted by the mistakes we make or we beat ourselves up with the feeling that we should be doing more for our kids, when the reality is that we're always doing the best we can with the resources and the knowledge we have.

If you're a parent, learn to accept that guilt is an inevitable part of child-rearing. But that doesn't mean you should wallow in it and get depressed. Just accept that some of your choices may cause some guilt and move on.

Remember that your child needs a healthy parent to get the best possible care, so your need for sleep, food and self-care is every bit as important as your child's.

One of the best ways of caring for your child is by ensuring that your guilt does not stop you from taking care of your own needs as a human being.

CHAPTER
Five

Don't Be Nice - Be Authentic

"The basic difference between being assertive and being aggressive is how our words and behavior affect the rights and well-being of others".

—Sharon Anthony Bower

Almost all women of my generation were brought up to be 'nice girls' – to not argue and be pleasant and pleasing, even at the **cost of our own self-esteem.**

But every time we did not speak up for ourselves, every time we kept quiet when we should have spoken up, we felt a little worse about ourselves.

And that little girl inside felt more and more lost in an adult body that did not protect her needs or stand up for her rights.

As women, we are taught to repress our emotions because they make other people uncomfortable – particularly men.

But your emotions are not bad. They are your guidance system, your compass to navigate the world. They tell you what things or actions are safe or harmful for you.

Few of us have learned **healthy ways of standing up for ourselves.** We harbor years of resentment and anger that end up sabotaging and damaging our relationships, all because we could not speak up when we needed to.

Repressing an emotion will only cause it to come up later in unhealthy or self-sabotaging ways.

Perhaps your anger forced you to rebel in your teenage years by doing things your parents disapproved of. Maybe you chose a husband or boyfriend who is wrong for you in an attempt to punish your parents for forcing their will on you.

There are **healthier ways to express emotions** that can change the course of our relationships and our lives.

A truly empowered woman does not feel the need to be either nice or nasty. She is real, authentic and can express who she is and how she feels in a calm, non-harming way.

She has learned ways to communicate that preserve the dignity of all concerned, so that her interactions create win-win situations that are acceptable to all.

When she faces abusive or unacceptable behavior, she **calmly and firmly sets boundaries** for what is and is not acceptable in her world.

For example, when someone puts you down or says something that makes you feel bad, you can choose to pretend that everything is ok and feel bad about not standing up for yourself.

Or you could choose to say, "Ouch! That hurt. I will not let you speak to me like that." When you give yourself the permission to be real, you will find it much easier to express yourself freely, without holding back.

Assertiveness is one skill that every woman must learn if she wants to be able to express her emotions in an authentic and non-harmful way.

Learn ways to be assertive, and keep practicing them with everyone you meet - from your rickshaw driver to your boss to your mother-in-law.

Even if it comes out as more aggressive than assertive the first few times, forgive yourself. Accept it as a learning experience and send yourself a mental memo that you'll do it differently the next time.

As with any skill, **assertive and authentic communication** takes practice. Do it more often and you'll get better at it.

CHAPTER
Six

Teach People How to Treat You

"We teach people how to treat us," said Dr Philip McGraw.

By tolerating behavior that does not respect your needs, you are allowing people to treat you in unacceptable ways.

When you **allow your family to take you for granted** as the one who always picks up after them, you're not allowing them the benefit of learning to do things for themselves.

When you do this with your children and spouse, you will not only end up feeling exploited, unappreciated and drained, but also allow them to believe that your needs are not important to you - and hence, not worthy of their consideration.

Only you can decide what you will tolerate and what you won't. This is something I had to learn the hard way too.

As a sensitive, empathic woman, my need for solitude happens to be greater than that of many other people, and I have had to exercise my right to my own space with a number of people in my life.

We need to **accept that our needs are not abnormal** just because they are different from the needs of others.

It depends on your unique personality, temperament and profession.

As a writer, my need to work alone a lot of the time meshes perfectly with my introverted personality; writing is, by nature, a solitary pursuit.

It took me years of believing I was flawed to finally realize that my needs are not unusual, and that I must respect them if I am to work and function at optimal levels.

I had to learn to set limits for how much time I spend around other people, and to **be politely firm when those boundaries were crossed**.

For you, it may be different. You may be more extroverted and need more time around others. You may find it hard to explain to an introverted husband why you need to spend so much time with your friends.

The idea is not to force others to live according to your standards. Nor am I recommending that you never try anything new or outside your comfort zone.

All you need to do is establish what works for you, and help those close to you accept you for who you are.

If you've been facing conflict in your relationships because one of you is more introverted or extroverted than the other, I highly recommend you take the Myers-Briggs Type Indicator® (MBTI®) assessment test.

This test was derived from the work of Carl Jung, and is a psychometric questionnaire designed to measure psychological preferences in how people perceive the world and make decisions.

You can either visit a qualified psychologist to understand your MBTI® personality type or use a **free MBTI® test online** (most of which happen to be pretty accurate).

Once you know your personality type, you can read more about it at **PersonalityPage.com** or just Google your type for more information.

For example, my type is INFP, so I would type "INFP" into Google to read more about it.

Understanding your own personality will help you appreciate why you are the way you are, and accept your own needs so you can teach your family and friends to respect them.

When you know your personality type, it becomes much easier to explain to your family and friends why you would prefer to read a book or watch a movie than go to a noisy party.

And once your family understands that this is your nature and this is what makes you happiest, they should respect it.

Besides issues related to your personality, you will also encounter situations at work and home where you have to set standards for the sort of behavior that makes you uncomfortable or unhappy.

DON'T FEEL GUILTY WHILE SETTING NEW STANDARDS FOR WHAT YOU WILL TOLERATE.

It is better to let others know what's on and what's not on, before they try to get you to do something that goes against your values or morals.

When you give in and do something that makes you uncomfortable, you will end up feeling unhappy with yourself and disgusted with your inability to stand up for your own values.

You can prevent this from happening by understanding what your standards are and making them clear to all concerned.

Not setting standards for acceptable behavior is one of the primary reasons for misunderstanding and conflict in relationships.

Whether it is that demanding client who wants you to do more than she is paying for, or your husband trying to get you to do something in the bedroom that makes you uncomfortable, **you need to be able to say "No" kindly and firmly, without anger or disrespect.**

CHAPTER
Seven

*Be Clear About What You
Can Give*

There are times when it is not enough just to set limits. Once you have set standards for what you will tolerate (and what you won't), you must let people know what they can (and can't) expect from you.

If, like most of us, you have a **hard time saying, "No" outright**, a good way to put it might be to say, "No I can't do that, but I can do this." That way the other person does not have to feel rejected.

For instance, if your mother or mother-in-law expects you to take care of her guests all by yourself while you are juggling work assignments and managing your kids' studies, you may have to be clear about just how much you are willing to do.

You might offer to cook for them but not to clean up afterwards or entertain them. Whatever you decide, make it clear so there are no unrealistic expectations or misunderstandings.

When **dealing with demanding clients** you could say something like, "No, I do not offer those services with this package, but if you upgrade to the Gold package, they will be included, or you could pay to have a package customized for you."

When you are clear with others about what they can expect from you, they will respect you for your honesty and for respecting yourself enough not to give in to their demands and expectations.

CHAPTER
Eight

Live From Your Heart

When you're attempting to bring more sanity into your life, you need to know exactly what that means to you.

Does it mean being less exhausted, less stressed, happier and more contented? Or does it mean **having more time and energy for your passions**, hobbies and leisure activities?

Does that mean having a few more hours in the day to -

- Write a blog
- Paint a watercolor
- Follow a creative pursuit
- Watch a movie
- Spend time with friends, or
- Plan your dream vacation
- Work on your business
- Play a sport
- Volunteer with a charity
- Mentor a young person

This is something only you can decide, based on your deepest, heart-felt desires. Today, women have fewer limitations on what they can do, so the only limits you have are the ones you place on yourself.

When deciding what you want to do with your life (or your spare time) you need to listen to your heart, not your head.

Your heart will tell you what you truly desire and what truly nurtures you, while your head will only argue for your limitations.

When you want to **live from your heart and follow your passions**, you must get rid of limitations – or at least pretend that they do not exist for now.

Do the small exercise below to understand your heart's desires. Write down the answers to these questions on a separate sheet of paper, without thinking about it too much.

Just let your pen flow and write the first thing that comes into your mind and makes you feel good when you think about it.

- What would I do right now if I had absolutely nothing stopping me?
- What do I dream of doing whenever I am seeking an escape?
- What did I enjoy doing most as a child between the ages of 7 and 14?

The idea is not just to learn what your heart desires, but also to open up the possibility of it actually happening by declaring it to the Universe.

You don't need to know *HOW* it will happen, only *WHAT* you want and *WHY* you want it.

Declare it and allow yourself to dream the dreams that you set aside to serve your family and career, and you may soon find yourself actually living them.

When you learn to live from the heart, you will feel more confident in your ability to make better choices for yourself.

In becoming a more fulfilled person, you will also be able to deal better with the minor irritations and triggers in your life and see them for what they really are – **lessons sent to help you learn how to treat yourself better.**

"Risk! Risk anything! Care no more for the opinions of others, for those voices. Do the hardest thing on earth for you. Act for yourself. Face the truth."

—Katherine Mansfield, Author

CHAPTER
Nine

Choose Happiness

I was once doing a meditation where I saw my inner child, the little girl inside me, and she was smiling at me and said, "I love you." That was when I realized I'm truly happy.

Every moment that I can, I decide to **think empowering thoughts**, and I know there is almost nothing that is worth losing my peace of mind over. But it was not always this way for me.

It's been a long journey for me to get to this day, and I still have my moments of stress, of angst, of anger…

But happiness is a feeling that permeates every area of my life, making even these momentary lapses bearable.

The first time I learned that I could **CHOOSE TO BE HAPPY** was in a book by Richard Carlson titled, "Shortcut Through Therapy: Ten Principles of Growth-Oriented, Contented Living".

I read this book more than once, sometime after I was widowed, when I was trying to regain my bearings and create a new identity as a single mother.

At the time, I was very stuck in my **victim mindset** and it had never really occurred to me that we can choose our own thoughts or choose to be happy.

Over the years, I learned that happy people are that way mainly because they choose to be that way - to **think thoughts that empower them**, ask empowering questions about their lives and because they have decided that almost nothing in life is worth losing your peace of mind over.

And I decided that was how I wanted to be. I learned that even death and loss cannot take away our peace of mind permanently, if we choose not to let them. It's a good way to be!

I hope you'll reach Richard Carlson's book and realize that you too can choose your thoughts every moment of every day.

At every point in your life, you have a choice – to choose a thought that empowers you, or to choose a thought that disempowers you. Why not choose the one that empowers you?

It takes the same amount of energy, and the outcome of **choosing a happy thought** is that, if you do it enough times, you'll be on your way to **living a happier life.**

In your relationships, choosing a happier thought could mean reminding yourself that your spouse's preoccupation with his Smartphone is not evidence of his rejecting you, but only his need to be focused on his work and his ability to provide for you.

> *"It's not what happens to you,*
> *but how you react to it that matters."*
>
> *—Epictetus*

There is no
Perfect Life.
There are only
Perfect Moments

Priya Florence Shah

PriyaFlorence.com

CHAPTER
Ten

Choose Compassion

The definition of compassion according to the dictionary is, "Deep awareness of the suffering of another coupled with the wish to relieve it."

When you learn to see the troublemakers in your life as just people who are learning their own lessons - and helping us to learn ours - we can view them with compassion and as fellow-travelers on the journey of life.

Though the things they say and do may upset us sometimes, we can learn to detach from the messenger and choose to understand the message instead.

Compassion starts with self-compassion. As the Buddha said, we are the ones who need our own compassion the most.

When you learn to stop beating yourself up for the way you react to triggers and **look at your own wounded inner child with compassion**, you will be able to feel the same towards others and understand that they are not trying to hurt you, but are acting from their own pain.

What is the wounded child? It comes from the archetypal Jungian notion of the eternal child, and is the basis for what psychologists and self-help authors like Margaret Paul and John Bradshaw call the "inner child."

To explain in in short, most of us received some sort of negative messages or perhaps sustained trauma between the ages of 1 to 7 years. The wounded child is the inner child that carries our hurt and trauma. It is our job, as adults, to re-parent our inner child and heal the hurts of the past.

One of the books that helped me work on my inner child healing is Margaret Paul's book, *Inner Bonding: Becoming a Loving Adult to Your Inner Child*. I highly recommend it if you find yourself in codependent relationships that are hard for you to leave.

Don't Take Anything Personally

This is one of the four agreements in the book, *The Four Agreements: A Practical Guide to Personal Freedom* by Don Miguel Ruiz. He writes:

Nothing others do is because of you. What others say and do is a projection of their own reality, their own dream.

When you are immune to the opinions and actions of others, you won't be the victim of needless suffering. There is a huge amount of freedom that comes to you when you take nothing personally.

It's not easy advice to follow because most of us feel hurt or wounded by criticism.

While we can never really know the true motives behind someone else's criticism of us, what we do know is that people usually lash out at others because of their own pain.

As the saying goes, '**Hurt people hurt people.**' People who are in pain are the ones who cause pain to others.

Choosing to see others in this way can help you see them not as enemies, but as mirrors – **human beings we attract in order to heal our own wounded child**.

The best reason **not to take another person's behavior personally** is because their criticism or abuse is never about you. It's about them and their own emotional wounds. They are only projecting on others the things they hate about themselves.

This does not mean that you have to stay in an abusive situation out of compassion for your abuser - but to learn to have compassion for yourself and **remove yourself from that situation** out of compassion for your abuser.

Don't stay in a bad situation hoping for the other person to change. Perhaps it is your very presence that triggers your abuser's pain in some way.

The kindest, most compassionate thing you can do is to change your own attitude and your environment so that you can prevent the behaviour from recurring.

Remove yourself from the painful situation so you can see things from a distance, and you will be able to feel compassion for both yourself and the other person.

CHAPTER
Eleven

Learn to Be Happy Without A Man

This sound advice comes from relationship guru, John Gray, author of the best-selling book, "*Men are from Mars, Women are from Venus.*"

John Gray specializes in teaching couples to have healthy relationships. I heard him make this statement in an interview, and completely agree with it.

The fact is, women have been happy without men for thousands of years, in India and worldwide.

It is our male-dominated society that has convinced us that we are 'incomplete' without men, and that we cannot survive without them. But this is not true.

Before nuclear families existed and the tribal system went extinct, men spent more time with other men, and women spent more time with other women.

In many parts of Indian society, this is still true. Men hang out more with other men, and women with other women. We just have more in common, that's all.

Today, there is more divorce than ever because men and women are looking to each other for the support they were getting from their own gender all this time.

And we are realising that men can never really understand us the way another woman can.

I have learned that a woman must learn to be complete in herself BEFORE she can learn to depend on a man in a healthy way.

I remember a scene from the Hindi movie, '*Arth*', which left a deep impression on me as a young woman.

The film is about a young couple (played by Shabana Azmi and Kulbhushan Kharbanda) who get embroiled in a love triangle when the husband falls in love with an attractive and very insecure actress (played by the late Smita Patil).

The couple separate as a result and a distraught Shabana is courted by an attractive man (played by Raj Kiran) who falls in love with her and empathises with her situation.

The scene I remember most is at the end of the movie, where Shabana is playing joyfully with her maid's daughter, whom she has adopted (after the maid was incarcerated for killing her abusive husband).

Raj Kiran proposes to her in the scene and she refuses, not because she does not like him, **but because she has made peace with her situation, and refuses to let herself be defined by a man.**

If you have not seen that movie, watch it on YouTube, especially if you're an Indian woman. It is one of the classics of Hindi cinema, with superb performances by two of Bollywood's most accomplished actresses.

However, the point I'm trying to make here is that it is not easy for a woman in India to be powerful in what is still very much a man's world.

This, despite the fact that Indian women have been symbols of strength for millennia. Deities like Lakshmi, Saraswati, Parvati, Durga and even Kali are expressions of feminine power at its peak.

But, over the centuries, we have allowed ourselves to be convinced that we're less than men, and that our roles are limited to being a wife, mother, daughter or sister.

We have defined ourselves in relationship to other people, usually the men of the house or the tribe.

In order for this to change, Indian women have to **learn to become more independent** and to manage our expectations in relation to the people in our lives.

"Seeking love keeps you from the awareness that you already have it — that you are it."

—Byron Katie

CHAPTER
Twelve

Manage Your Expectations

"How wrong is it for a woman to expect the man to build the world she wants, rather than to create it herself?"

—*Anais Nin*

I have learned that the only person you can ever really, truly, expect anything from is yourself. And even we tend to let ourselves down now and then.

Most of our disillusionment and disappointment in relationships and life comes from **unrealistic expectations**.

From doing things for others expecting that they will do the same for us. From assuming that others can fulfill our unfulfilled desires.

Many arranged marriages in India work better than love marriages because the spouses have fewer expectations from each other. Unlike people who marry for love, they don't expect the other person to 'complete' them.

When you are expecting another person to 'complete' you, you're coming from a place of lack. It means you are not willing to take the responsibility to heal yourself and become whole.

If that is your attitude, you will always be disappointed with your relationships, because **no one can really 'complete' another person**. We are each responsible for our own healing and happiness.

The only way you can feel whole is by taking the responsibility to heal your childhood hurts and cultivate a relationship with the Divine in you.

When you connect with a source of abundant love that does not have to come from another human being, you will never experience scarcity of love.

You can then offer unconditional love to others without feeling needy or requiring them to love you in return.

Your relationships will then flow from a place of fullness and love, and your loved ones will cease to be burdened by your expectations.

Yes, we could blame our spouses for their excessive expectations too, but it only takes one person in a relationship to change in order for the entire relationship to be transformed.

When you come from a place of gratitude, not entitlement, and accept what your man has to offer without unrealistic expectations, he will be more than happy to make you happy.

On your part what you need to do is build a strong support system - starting with your Higher Self or Divine Connection, and extending to other women friends - so you can get the support you need without expecting your partner to fulfill all your needs.

"It is only when we no longer compulsively need someone that we can have a real relationship with them."

—Anthony Storr

CHAPTER
Thirteen

*Cultivate These 6 Forms
of Independence*

As a woman who's experienced her fair share of personal tragedy and failed relationships, I feel very strongly that a woman should be **completely independent** of her man.

I don't mean that you should never let a man do anything for you. **Independence to me means being able to take care of my own needs in a healthy manner, with or without a man.**

Independence promotes self-worth and self-esteem. Healthy, secure men are attracted to independent, confident women.

Independence also gives you the confidence to walk away from an unfulfilling or abusive relationship.

It's not empowering to be the "damsel in distress", waiting for a man to "rescue" you from your loneliness. Only insecure men like women who are clingy and dependent. And that's definitely not the sort of man you want to attract, is it?

There are **six forms of independence** every woman should cultivate:

1. Physical Independence

I have seen many **codependent women** fake illness (or choose to believe that they're ill) to get attention and get their family to take care of them.

Really, how empowering can it be to have someone else take care of all your physical needs?

Unless you suffer from a serious illness or disability, doing basic things like buying groceries, managing your bank accounts, and paying bills are things you should be able to do for yourself, even if you live with someone else.

Take responsibility for your own health and well-being. When you become a burden to others, you also make yourself vulnerable to abuse or abandonment.

2. Sexual Independence

Learning to pleasure oneself can be very empowering for a woman. Men do it all the time, so there's no reason why women can't.

If you can meet your own sexual needs in a healthy manner, you'll never have to settle for one-night stands or relationships that are demeaning.

Because of conditioning by family and society, many women are not even comfortable with exploring their own bodies. False beliefs about sex and our own bodies can lead to sexual incompatibility and unhappiness in marriage.

For the sake of your marriage and relationships, learn to get comfortable with your own body. If you know how to pleasure yourself, you can help your partner pleasure you better.

3. Financial Independence

Many women still expect a man to be the provider and a source of security. A man who has a home and car is seen as a better match than one who doesn't.

But like us women, men want to be loved for themselves, not for what they can give us.

If you depend on a man financially, you'll always be at his mercy, willing to tolerate abuse or disrespectful behaviour. Relationships built on a foundation of need are doomed to fail, or be unhappy for one or both people.

Unless you're taking care of the kids and the home – which is a job in itself - no woman should be financially dependent on a man.

At the very least, she should be educated or capable of using her skills and talents to stand on her own two feet, should the man walk out of the relationship or pass away.

Being **financially independent** enhances your own **self-worth**, and gives you the freedom to make better choices in relationships. You're less likely to tolerate disrespect or abuse if you know you can fend for yourself.

4. Emotional Independence

This is the ability to **deal with emotional issues and problems** on your own. If you act emotionally needy and clingy, you'll attract men who are insecure and controlling.

Neediness will not only attract potential abusers but will also drive away a good man looking for a strong, independent woman.

If you're having trouble meeting your own emotional needs, I recommend you read the book, *Inner Bonding: Becoming a Loving Adult to Your Inner Child* by Margaret Paul.

5. Spiritual Independence

A good man wants to be with an independent-thinking woman, not one who follows him around agreeing to everything he says.

Being an independent thinker means having the courage to stand by your beliefs, speak your mind, and follow the path that feels right for you.

It makes you less likely to attract a man who is controlling and tries to dictate what you should think, read or believe in.

6. Social Independence

I include here, one more form of independence suggested by Harsh Shrivastava.

"Women should have their own network (including online) of friends, advisers, guides, mentors, and even mentees – of both genders," says Harsh. "A woman should not depend only on relatives or her man's friends, but have her own set of people to lean on and learn from and have fun with."

I couldn't agree more!

Independence is attractive because it gives a woman the freedom to make better choices and enter a healthy, authentic, inter-dependent relationship on her own terms.

CHAPTER
Fourteen

Security Or Freedom?

Relationship experts state that feminine energy craves security (or the feeling of being cherished) and that masculine energy craves freedom (or the feeling of being respected).

But in today's world, women are expressing their desire for freedom and growth just as much as men. For women who love freedom, security can become a prison.

You have to remember that the more security you desire, the less freedom you will have. Conversely, the more freedom you desire, the less security you will have. You can't have both.

Also remember that the security we get from things and people outside of ourselves is an illusion. As with most emotional wounds, a **lack of security** comes from childhood conditioning, acquired in situations where we felt powerless or unsafe.

True security comes from having faith in a Higher Power.

If you have a strong inner sense of security and the certainty that you can rebuild your life, you could lose everything one day and still bounce back.

If you're a woman who loves her freedom, you need to know that it can be very empowering to get comfortable with uncertainty - with not needing to know what is going to happen next.

When you want to take your life to a new level, being comfortable with uncertainty is an attitude that will help you open up to new things and learn much faster than if you hold your security dear.

That way you get to **flow with whatever life has to offer** and be open to receiving the best it has in store for you.

"Those who surrender freedom for security
will not have, nor do they deserve, either one."

—Thomas Jefferson

CHAPTER
Fifteen

Step Out of
Your Comfort Zone

Growth involves discomfort. If you want to grow, you have to get comfortable with being uncomfortable, with stretching yourself, **trying new things**, going to new places, meeting new people.

You may have to do things that are not in your nature. You will experience fear, apprehension and anxiety.

"Whatever you fear most has no power -
it is your fear that has the power."

—Oprah Winfrey

Your ego will throw up all sorts of arguments about why you should stay small, not try anything new and stay within your comfort zone. Your ego wants to keep you safe - from embarrassment, from falling flat on your face, from failure.

But growing means taking risks, rising to a challenge, reaching new heights – and yes, even failing, falling flat and picking yourself up to start again.

The biggest regret you will have as you grow older is that you did not take more risks. Growth is what Spirit wants for you. So **step outside your comfort zone.** Do this regularly and often.

If you're an introvert, go out and meet people. Make friends with people you would not normally interact with. If you're afraid of heights, take a course in mountaineering, or try skydiving.

Learn a new skill. Try something you've never tried before.

Your greatest triumph lies just beyond your greatest fears.

CHAPTER
Sixteen

Face Your Fears

ational fears include those that are based on our instincts, like the fear of falling or the fear of predators (including the modern kind).

Irrational fears, like the fears of public speaking, meeting new people and asserting ourselves, are created by disempowering beliefs installed in childhood.

This is especially true in the case of Indian women, who invariably experience far more negative childhood conditioning than their male counterparts.

Rational fears help us care for our safety and avoid harm in a healthy way. It is definitely a good idea to pay attention to them.

For example, if you're walking home late at night and see a suspicious-looking man following you, it would be wise to pay attention to your fears and hail a cab or find a safer way home.

Irrational fears are the ones that hold us back from expressing our greatness and living a bigger life. When you learn to see a fear for what it is, you can choose to respond in a calmer and wiser way.

Irrational fears are the ones we must learn to disregard and move through. How do you move through a fear?

As the title of a well-known book says, *"Feel the Fear and Do it Anyway."* Pick up a copy and read it if you find that your fears have been ruling your life.

Remember that irrational fears are your ego's way of keeping you small. These fears are your mind's way of keeping you safe and protecting you from failure or looking foolish.

As a child, you may have felt safe listening to them. But, as an adult woman, you can talk to your ego as you would respond to a fearful adult who gives you 'well-meaning' advice.

Whenever a fearful or self-limiting thought comes into my mind, I reply, "Thank you for sharing. I know you mean well, but there is nothing to be afraid of now."

> *"You gain strength, courage, and confidence*
> *by every experience in which you really stop to*
> *look fear in the face. You must do the thing which*
> *you think you cannot do."*
>
> **—Eleanor Roosevelt**

CHAPTER
Seventeen

Live In The Now

Most of our anxiety and angst comes from focusing on either the past or the future. But worrying about a future that has not yet happened (and may never happen) is a waste of a perfectly good present.

"I've suffered a great many catastrophes in my life. Most of them never happened."

—Mark Twain

When you worry, you're creating a future that you don't want. Because as I will show you in another chapter, "Where attention goes, energy flows."

How you live and act in the present determines what your next moment will be like. If your words and actions are thoughtless, you will create pain for yourself and others.

If you want to create your best future, keep your focus on what you're doing and feeling now. That way you can choose to respond in a way that will make the next moment a good one.

Ever notice how, when you're focused on a task you enjoy, you very rarely allow any other thoughts to cross your mind?

This is called **mindfulness** – the practice of staying focused on the things that matter, from moment to moment.

My favourite ways of cultivating the practice of mindfulness are doing the work that I love, breathing practices (*Pranayama*) and meditation.

But, I have also taken mindfulness courses by Buddhist teachers like Pema Chödrön. If you can find a mindfulness practice that works for you, cultivate it.

We are only at peace when we are focused on the present moment. And NOW is really all there is.

"Not only are you responsible for your life,
but doing the best at this moment puts you in
the best place for the next moment."

—Oprah Winfrey

We all know what it's like to be triggered — to have said something we wish we hadn't, or reacted in a way that wasn't helpful. What if there was a way to interrupt our knee-jerk responses?

In her course, The Freedom to Choose Something Different, Pema Chödrön offers a liberating teaching called *shenpa* for disarming reactivity, to help you break free of old habits and negative patterns.

Her course will assist you in accessing your ability to make better choices in your daily life. You'll understand not only what it means to be hooked to old patterns and habits, but also how you can go beyond them.

If you've been struggling with reacting in less than ideal ways to various situations, whether you lash out, write nasty letters, or shut down with people in your life, her course will teach you how to change those patterns and react in a more grounded, and calmer way.

CHAPTER
Eighteen

Surrender To Faith

No doubt, having a sense of control over our lives is empowering. But what happens when something takes away that feeling?

It could be a loved one's death, the break-up of a relationship, losing money in your investments, finding out that your child is autistic...

Whatever it is, if you think you can control everything that happens to you and your loved ones, you are creating a very unhappy existence for yourself and for those around you.

Give Up The Illusion Of Control

Control freaks are some of the unhappiest people in the world because they believe that everything must go according to their plans.

And when it doesn't, which is invariably the case, they shake their heads in disbelief and feel powerless.

Giving up control does not mean that we just sit and let our lives pass by. It means we do the work required to achieve our goals, but **detach from the outcome**.

There are some things you can control – like the actions you need to take to achieve a result - and others you can't control, like the result itself.

When you begin to feel powerless over the things that you cannot control, remember the Serenity Prayer. It goes like this:

Grant me the serenity to accept the things I cannot change,

The courage to change the things I can,

And the wisdom to know the difference.

You can put your best effort into your actions, but the result depends on more factors than just your efforts. The results can either be less than you hoped for, or they can surpass your wildest dreams.

Accept that you can control your actions, but let go of the outcome.

From my Taoist teachers, I have learned that **giving up control allows you to flow with life** and open up to receiving all that the Universe has to offer you.

When you realize that control is just an illusion created by the ego and your own fears, and you decide to stop trying to control everyone and everything, you open yourself up to the limitless possibilities that the Universe has for you.

Often, we just need to get out of our own way to allow something better in.

For all you know, that tiny business you remain so obsessed with could be preventing you from creating a million-dollar empire you are capable of creating, or from penning the best-seller you always dreamed of writing.

Give the Universe the chance to act on your behalf instead of trying to have it your way.

"The Universe has imagined it even better than you have."

—Unknown

Instead of Control - which comes from Fear - learn to have Faith that things always turn out for the best, **even if it does not seem like that right now.**

FEAR AND FAITH CANNOT COEXIST IN OUR MINDS. WE CAN EITHER HAVE ONE OR THE OTHER.

As women, we are more intuitive than men and have the ability to easily connect to our Divine source of wisdom and well-being.

The ones who contribute the most to the world, are also the ones most connected to their own source of Divine wisdom.

You have the same potential to share your unique gifts with the world – all you need to do is to start cultivating a spiritual life and listen to your intuition.

As children, we come into this world knowing that we are deserving of love… until the judgments and actions of our parents and caregivers tell us otherwise.

As we grow older, we have to fight the conditioning of our parents and the residual hurt of our **childhood wounds** in order to believe that we are loved and lovable.

Even if the love of another human being is deficient, Divine love is not.

When you connect to your own unique source of Divine Love and guidance, you will not only cease to be needy for human love and affection, but will be able to give and receive it in a healthier way.

Whether you call it Jesus, Allah, Bhagwan, the Universe, Source Energy or the Force (thank you, George Lucas), it's all the same.

Cultivating your faith in a Higher Power gives you the assurance that you are always loved unconditionally.

"You are loved. All is Well."

—*Abraham-Hicks*

CHAPTER
Nineteen

Attract More Abundance In Your Life

"It is a kind of spiritual snobbery that makes people think they can be happy without money."

—Albert Camus

Can you fill up another person's cup when your own is empty?

How can you give to another person when you are struggling with resources in your own life? And why do we feel that we have to have less so that others can have more?

Many Indians are brought up with the conditioning that an abundance of material wealth is bad or only available by illegal means - and that rich people are shallow and superficial.

The truth is that money only makes you more of who you already are. If you act like a jerk when you're poor, you'll act like a jerk when you're rich.

As Wayne Dyer so aptly put it, "Circumstances do not make a man, they reveal him."

Remember that some of the richest people on Earth - like Bill Gates, Warren Buffet, Azim Premji, and Oprah Winfrey - are the most generous with their money and donate the most to charity.

"Poverty is a way of living and thinking, and not just a lack of money or things."

—Eric Butterworth

A poverty or scarcity mindset can also come from the belief that we are not deserving of good things and that we have to suffer and work hard to attract good things.

The wise ones know that there is enough in the Universe for everyone. Scarcity is a human condition created by fear.

Abundance flows to those who believe that they deserve it and are most aligned with their life purpose.

Abundance is not just about money. It is about attracting to yourself everything that you desire to have in your life – loving relationships, meaningful work, a happy family, good health, a beautiful home...

When you **allow yourself to receive abundance in all its forms**, knowing that it is your birthright, you make it safe for others to receive from their own source of abundance.

"The world is full of abundance and opportunity,
but far too many people come to the fountain of life with a
sieve instead of a tank car... a teaspoon instead of a steam
shovel. They expect little and as a result they get little."

—Ben Sweetland

When you have an **abundance mindset**, you do not cling to the things and people you have in your life because of your fear of losing them.

You trust that even if you don't get something or someone you want, it is because you are destined to attract something or someone better.

And when your life is full of abundance, you can give fully and whole-heartedly to others from a place of true giving.

Here are 7 lessons to attract more abundance in your life:

1. Where Attention Goes, Energy Flows

This is a lesson I learned from my beloved teachers, *Abraham-Hicks*, who were teaching the Law of Attraction 20 years before *The Secret* was released.

It sounds deceptive in its simplicity – and that's because it is actually so hard to do. To understand the concept better, try a simple exercise:

DON'T think of an elephant.

The curious thing is that, once you have invited the elephant into your consciousness, it becomes all you can think of.

And that is how it is with things we DON'T want.

The more we try **NOT TO** think of them (because of the pain or discomfort they cause), the more we think of them, and the more we invite them into our consciousness… and our lives.

> *"Whatever I am looking at,*
> *I am including in my vibration.*

> **—Abraham**

If you want to stop thinking of what you don't want, all you need to do is practice focusing your thoughts on what you <u>DO WANT</u>.

Why is it so important to do this? Because as many wise teachers of the past have noted, <u>**we become what we think about**</u>.

Your thoughts manifest your reality. And if you think unhappy thoughts, who will you be? That's right - a miserable person.

It's not about pretending that you have no issues or challenges. The truth is that the only people who have no challenges are the ones in the cemetery.

But you CAN attract good things into your life by taking your focus OFF what you don't want and putting it ON what you want instead.

Let me repeat this, because it is a practice that has transformed my own life:

Take your focus <u>OFF</u> the things and people you don't want, and put it <u>ON</u> the things you do want.

It's not easy at first, because your 'Monkey Mind' will keep going right back to those unhappy thoughts.

When that happens, don't beat yourself up for it. Just let the unhappy thought go and bring your focus back to the happy thought.

In the book, *Ask And It Is Given: Learning to Manifest Your Desires*, Abraham-Hicks teach 22 processes for shifting your thoughts from those with a lower vibration to ones with a higher vibration. You'll definitely find one or more processes that work for you in this must-read book.

The way we choose to think is a merely a habit - and as with any other habit, it can be changed with practice and commitment. It is a commitment worth making to yourself.

2. Find Things To Appreciate

"Appreciation in advance brings everything you want to you.

—Abraham-Hicks

One of the techniques that they teach to **attract more of what you want in your life**, is learning to appreciate what you already have.

This is one of the best attitudes to cultivate and the best time to cultivate it is when you feel least appreciative of anything.

Finding things to appreciate, even when you are not feeling it, allows you to keep your focus on what you want and take it off the things you don't want.

You cannot be in a place of appreciation and complaining at the same time. You can do either one or the other.

For instance, you can either appreciate the things you love about your partner or complain about his failings. Whatever you give attention to will become the dominant experience in your relationship.

Appreciation for what you have (or desire to have) aligns you with the energy of the Universe and allows the things you want to flow to you easily.

So, the more you appreciate, the more there is to appreciate.

"We can always choose to perceive things differently.
You can focus on what's wrong in your life,
or you can focus on what's right."

—Marianne Williamson

3. Cultivate Empowering Beliefs

"What we think, we become.

—Buddha

Your life is a reflection of the beliefs you hold. If you say that you want to succeed but your subconscious beliefs don't match your desires, it won't happen.

You need to become conscious of which beliefs are holding you back and clear them from your system.

As geek-speak goes, "Garbage In, Garbage Out". What you put into your mind, you get back again.

If you fill your mind with endless negativity from soap operas, commercials and the mass media, your life will become a replica of what you see there.

Far too many Indian women regularly sacrifice precious time and mental bandwidth on the altar of meaningless passive entertainment – and they are paying the price.

If you want to have empowering beliefs, only expose yourself to empowering thoughts.

Read inspiring books, subscribe to inspiring newsletters, stop watching TV (yes, it can be done) or watch less of it, and spend more time in the company of people who inspire you.

Which brings me to the next point…

4. Be Mindful of the Company You Keep

You're the average of the five people you spend the most time with, said Jim Rohn.

If you want to be more successful, hang out with people you admire and want to emulate, not with those who are in the same boat.

Success can be scary for some people, and the journey to the top can be lonely – especially for a woman. Find a mentor and ask him or her to coach you.

A very apt quote I read is *"Your companions are like the buttons on an elevator. They will either take you up or they will take you down."*

Spend your time with people who elevate you, not those who pull you down.

How can you tell if a friend is pulling you down? Well, trust the way you feel when you're around them.

If your mood is considerably dampened when they're around, they may not be giving you the kind of nurturing that you need.

Even if you can't avoid such people entirely, **seek out others who are more positive** and spend time with them. Learn how they think, how they live and see the world through their eyes.

There is a significant difference in mindset between those who are poor, those who are just getting by and those who are thriving.

To up-level your life, you need to not only **work on your own beliefs**, but also understand the beliefs, mindset and lives of those you admire and wish to emulate.

Cultivate relationships with people whom you want to be like. You can pay to be part of a community, a networking group, or a mastermind group of individuals who are more successful than you.

If you don't have any such people in your life right now, you can make a good start by **reading the biographies of great men and women.**

Books can become our best friends in such a situation, because they give us a glimpse into the lives of great people we may never have a chance to meet.

"By associating with wise people you will become wise yourself."

—Menander

5. Never Apologise for Your Success

Your family and friends may not be supportive of your goals and plans. Learn to draw strong boundaries with those you cannot avoid.

Explain to those who offer 'well-meaning' advice that, while you appreciate their input, you would like the freedom to make your own mistakes.

Never put yourself down or underplay your achievements just to make the other person feel better.

"When we let our own light shine, we unconsciously give other people permission to do the same."

—Marianne Williamson

As you grow in success, you will face resistance from those who are threatened by change or are fearful that they will lose you.

This is where many of us women self-sabotage and choose to stay small – when we fear the loss of our significant relationships.

But I've learned that the ones who have your best interests at heart will support your growth anyway.

And the ones who don't? Well, you could explain it to them gently, but understand that **you are not responsible**

for their fears, so **don't hold yourself back** because of them.

Successful people become easy targets of those who are afraid to let their own light shine. **Don't take their criticism, jealousy or envy personally**.

Know that it is about them, not you. They are just projecting their own fears and limiting beliefs on to you.

Stay focused on your goals and your vision and you will attract more people who think like you. You may lose some friends, but you will **gain many new ones who are more supportive of the New You**.

> *"How does one become a butterfly?" she asked.*
> *"You must want to fly so much that you are willing*
> *to give up being a caterpillar."*
>
> **—Anonymous**

6. Invest In Yourself

Invest time and money in learning and growing. Take courses, learn new skills. It will make a huge difference to your life and success, whether you have a business or career.

If you're a businesswoman, you will attract better quality clients who are also willing to invest in their own businesses and pay higher fees.

The logic is, "Why would anyone invest in someone who is not willing to invest in themselves?" Right?

If you have a job, your knowledge will help you stand out in the workplace and get you noticed by your employers.

You might hesitate because of the expense of spending on courses. But, I assure you, that if you apply the knowledge you acquire, you will more than recover your expenses, by increasing the value you offer your clients or employers.

Here's an important rule of money:

What you earn is in direct proportion to the value you add to people's lives.

If you want to be more successful in your business or career, learn to increase the value you offer your clients or employers.

When you learn to BE more and GIVE more, you will ATTRACT more abundance into your own life.

"Formal education will make you a living; self-education will make you a fortune."

—*Jim Rohn*

7. Have Fun

If you ask me the purpose of life, I would quote my teachers, Abraham-Hicks, in saying that: **The Basis of your life is Freedom; the Purpose of your life is Joy.**

Abundance is not just about money, it's also about joy and fulfillment. If what you're doing does not bring you joy, ask why that is and what you can do to change it.

Perhaps you want to do work that is more meaningful, even if you earn less money. Spend time in Nature, take time off from work.

Do whatever nurtures your spirit, whether that involves travel, hobbies or just spending time with friends and family with whom you can have a good laugh.

> *"Don't take life too seriously.*
> *You'll never get out of it alive."*
>
> **—Elbert Hubbard**

CHAPTER
Twenty

Are These "Brules" Ruining Your Life?

Vishen Lakhiani of MindValley, a personal development company, introduced a new term in his book, *The Code of the Extraordinary Mind.*

The term is *'brules'* - **or "bullshit rules."**

As Vishen writes, "We all absorb the cultural norms of our society, but we often forget to question whether these are serving us — or limiting us."

He goes on to explain why these *"brules"* are so dangerous, and how to begin questioning the unconscious, insidious limiting beliefs you may be holding.

As someone who's always been a non-conformist, I found this term especially fitting to describe the rules of society I discarded for the sake of my mental peace many years ago.

To give you the short version:

- I stopped practicing religion when I was 16

- Fell in love with and married a man outside my community (he passed away at the age of 37)

- Left a career in scientific research to follow my passion for writing

- Married again and divorced because I don't feel the need to conform to anyone else's expectations of me

Not needing to conform to society's expectations has given me the **freedom and independence** to choose my own path and do what I love with my life.

And I wish every person in the world felt as free to follow their heart and intuition and do what's right for them.

If you find yourself **burdened by the weight of other people's expectations**, here are some of the *Brules* – or bullshit rules - of society that may be ruining your life.

1. The *brule* of success

Many parents - and I'm looking at you, Indian parents – believe that their kids need to become doctors or engineers to be happy.

This brule is hurting so many sensitive and creative youngsters who end up committing suicide because they bought into their parents' unhealthy expectations of them.

I have met many engineers who are much happier in fields such as event management where they feel free to express their creativity.

I was so gratified when that Aamir Khan movie, 3 Idiots, showed how it's acceptable for someone to leave engineering to pursue his dream of being a photographer.

I would even go so far as to state that you don't need a higher education to be successful, because there exist so many examples of wildly successful people who didn't even complete high school.

So, please let your child follow their passions. Perhaps they want to be a musician, an artist or an actor or – Heaven forbid – an entrepreneur.

Grant them the time and the freedom to experiment, make mistakes and find their life purpose.

Just don't try to realize your unfulfilled aspirations through your kids by forcing them to become a lawyer or doctor. You should know that these are some of the careers with the highest rates of depression and suicide.

2. The *brule* of marriage

The belief that you need to be married to be happy is one of the biggest bullshit rules, in my book. First of all, I do not buy into the *brule* that marriage is a sacred bond.

Early humans had no concept of marriage. Most of them only paired up long enough to care for their offspring for a certain number of years after which they would move on.

The "love hormone," oxytocin, creates a pair bond that only lasts for about 4 years or so in humans. Which is why the concept of the "4 or 7 year itch" exists – the knowledge that couples often stray after 7 years of being married.

Because that's when the biochemical fog of the love hormone finally wears off and we see each other as we really are. As this article in Scientific American notes:

The four-year divorce peak among modern humans may represent the remains of an ancestral reproductive strategy to stay bonded at least long enough to raise a child through infancy and early toddlerhood.

Thus, we may have a natural weak point in our unions. By understanding this susceptibility in our human nature, we might become better able to anticipate, and perhaps be able to avoid, the four-year itch.

For me, this puts paid to the notion that humans are biologically designed to bond for life.

Another objection that I have to the bullshit rule of marriage is that in early marriages, women were little more than property. Unfortunately, many marriage contracts of today seem to contain the same connotations.

Women are often required to change their names, give up their careers, and even their identities, in favour of the man. A woman is rarely ever seen as an equal partner in marriage. It's one of the many reasons I prefer being single.

Don't get me wrong. I'm not against relationships. I love being with my partner of many years (who also happens to be my ex-husband). We're the best of friends and have a great deal of mutual respect and caring for each other.

But I hate being anyone's "wife" because that word has so many negative connotations for me. And considering how Indian wives are treated by their in-laws, that's not totally unfounded either.

Yes, there are many truly happy marriages, but they exist because those couples have the **emotional**

intelligence, the relationship skills and the willingness to grow and evolve as partners.

Most of us in our 20s do not have the skills to be in a committed relationship, so this *brule* about marriage imprisons millions of people in unhappy marriages.

I believe marriage should be a choice, not the norm. And it should be easy to leave an unhappy marriage, kids or not.

So, don't fall for the *brule* that you need to be married to be happy. Being in a relationship is great. But, for women especially, marriage can be counter-productive to happiness.

3. The *brule* of having kids

The same *brule* applies to the belief that you need to have kids to be happy. In my case, I had a child because I always saw myself as a mother and I really love being a mom.

But not every man or woman likes kids or wants to be a parent. Nor should they be forced to do something they are not suited for just because of this bullshit rule.

That only ends up creating **unhappy, traumatized kids who are scarred for life by the realization that they were not wanted**.

So if you don't want kids – and this is for you young people out there – you don't need to have them.

Don't give into family and peer pressure to reproduce. With 7.3 billion humans on this planet, it's not like you'll be contributing to the survival of humanity.

4. The *brule* of separateness

Another *brule* – and this is a biggie – is the illusion of separateness.

The illusion that we belong to separate religions, countries, cultures, castes, income, class, etc. is just another brule.

And it serves only those who want to divide and rule us.

In truth, we are all part of one consciousness. There is no us or them.

Yes, religions, dogmas, belief systems, cultural constructs are all part of the diversity of human experience.

But you need to challenge and question a belief system if it tells you that you are more or less than any other human being on this planet.

5. The *brule* of monogamy

So I left the most controversial *brule* for last. Now, many of us are aware that monogamy is not the norm in human society.

We have heard of polygamy, polyandry, group marriage and many other forms of human pair bonding. The hippies lived in communes and practiced free love.

There is nothing right or wrong with any of it. It's all a personal choice and that is exactly what monogamy is – a personal choice.

When we enter a committed relationship, we choose to be monogamous. **When we turn it into an expectation or a moral judgment - that's when it results in unhappiness.**

Most humans are not monogamous by nature, which accounts for all the time we spend in marriage counseling and divorce courts.

All I can say about this *brule* is that, if you choose to be monogamous and want to avoid heartbreak, make sure your partner and you are both on the same page.

I believe that, if we want to be happy, we should question EVERYTHING, refuse to accept another person's view of the world as our own and choose to live our lives guided by our own INTUITION.

If you believe you need permission to do that, the next chapter will show you what's possible when you discard conventions to live the life you were created for.

CHAPTER
Twenty One
Embrace Your 'Weirdness'

"Here's to the crazy ones. The misfits. The rebels. The troublemakers. The round pegs in the square holes. The ones who see things differently. They're not fond of rules. And they have no respect for the status quo. You can quote them, disagree with them, glorify or vilify them. About the only thing you can't do is ignore them. Because they change things. They push the human race forward. And while some may see them as the crazy ones, we see genius. Because the people who are crazy enough to think they can change the world, are the ones who do."

—Rob Siltanen (for Apple's "Think Different" commercial)

What would the world be without the misfits, the rebels, the square pegs in round holes? It is visionaries like Steve Jobs who changed our view of the world today.

It is the ones with 'disabilities' like Leonardo Da Vinci, Albert Einstein, Richard Branson, John Lennon, Pablo Picasso and Thomas Edison (**all of whom were dyslexic**) who have transformed the world with their vision, talent and brilliance.

What if their disabilities had been weeded out of them so that they 'fit in' better into an education system that kills creativity and genius?

Would the world have benefited from the gifts that only they could have contributed?

Or would they have been turned into dumbed-down clones of everyone who graduates from the academic assembly lines that pass for schools today?

These views may be somewhat radical, but I believe that these geniuses - and many others - made the contributions they did **because they opted out of the game.**

They chose not to do what everyone else did simply because they were not cut out for it.

Instead of focusing their attention on their disability – something that was not even diagnosed back then - they developed their own unique talents... and changed the way we experience the world.

Today, a diagnosis of disability can brand a child for life, causing endless embarrassment and destroying her fragile self-esteem in a world that stresses academic achievements over creative genius.

I believe that when you embrace your 'weirdness', your 'disabilities' or your own unique gifts that the Universe has bestowed on you, you teach all of us to see the world through different eyes.

When you share the vision that comes through your own unique lens with the rest of the world, you make all of our lives richer.

So don't let anyone make you feel 'less-than' just because you're not academically inclined or cannot fulfill your parents' unfulfilled aspirations. You may be destined to be the next Picasso, and to add to the beauty of all our lives.

To me the story of the Cracked Pot illustrates this best:

A water bearer in China had two large pots, each hung on the ends of a pole which he carried across his neck. One of the pots had a crack in it, while the other pot was perfect and always delivered a full portion of water.

At the end of the long walk from the stream to the House, the cracked pot arrived only half full. For a full two years this went on daily, with the bearer delivering only one and a half pots full of water to his house.

Of course, the perfect pot was proud of its perfection and accomplishments. But the poor cracked pot was ashamed of its own imperfection, and miserable that it was able to accomplish only half of what it had been made to do.

After two years of what it perceived to be bitter failure, it spoke to the water bearer one day by the stream.

"I am ashamed of myself, and I want to apologize to you. I have been able to deliver only half my load because this crack in my side causes water to leak out all the way back to your house. Because of my flaws, you have to do all of this work, and you don't get full value from your efforts," the pot said.

The bearer said to the pot, "Did you notice that there were flowers only on your side of the path, but not on the other pot's side? That's because I have always known about your flaw. So I planted flower seeds on your side of the path, and every day while we walk back, you've watered them. For two years I have been able to pick these beautiful flowers to decorate the table. Without you being just the way you are, there would not be this beauty to grace the house?"

CHAPTER
Twenty Two
Care For Your Body & Mind

"To keep the body in good health is a duty, otherwise we shall not be able to keep our mind strong and clear."

—Buddha

Your body is your Divine vessel – it harbours your soul. You have a Divine duty to care for your body just as much as you care for your soul.

Many Indian women stop caring for themselves after they have kids and reach middle-age. I've been guilty of this myself. But the way you look tells the world a lot about your self-esteem.

You don't have to go overboard and spend thousands on beauty treatments, because looking good is an inside job. If you feel good about yourself, you will naturally take pride in your appearance.

You don't have to become a fitness freak. Just nurture yourself by eating well and not too much, getting regular exercise and **maintaining a healthy weight**.

Do what is right for you, not what works for others. Everyone's body is unique and we each need to find a regimen that works best for us.

Also remember that a lot of health issues stem from our beliefs. That's why some people fall ill easily and others remain healthy, even when exposed to the same conditions.

Cultivating empowering beliefs and thoughts has been shown to have a significant impact on our health, and even to **heal terminal illnesses like cancer**.

If you want to learn more about the mind-body connection, I recommend reading the book, *You Can Heal Your Life* by Louise Hay.

"Wellness that is being allowed - or the wellness that is being denied - is all about the mindset, the mood, the attitude, the practiced thoughts. There is not one exception, in any human or beast; because, you can patch them up again and again, and they will just find another way of reverting back to the natural rhythm of their mind. Treating the body really is about treating the mind. It is all psychosomatic. Every bit of it, no exceptions."

—Esther Hicks

CHAPTER
Twenty Three

Seek Help When You Need It

If you go through life without self-inquiry and self-awareness, you will come up against the same obstacles time and time again, and attract the same disempowering situations until you decide to do the work required to heal your wounds.

There is no shame in admitting we need help. Every person on Earth has issues that need healing and there are many healing modalities you can try.

There is no 'one-size-fits-all' solution. Different methods work for different people. Some healing modalities that have worked for me include:

Meditation

Mindfulness

Hypnosis

Emotional Freedom Technique (EFT)

Reiki

Psychotherapy or Counselling

Traumas and disempowering beliefs create energy blockages in our body that prevent us from reaching our full potential.

If you have faced serious trauma or problems in your life and need professional help, don't hesitate to consult a qualified psychologist or an energy healer.

Better yet, learn to heal yourself. We all have the ability to do it and it's just one more way to take care of ourselves.

It helps to have a tribe or community of close friends with whom you can unburden yourself whenever a crisis looms or when you just need to talk.

"Healing may not be so much about getting better,
as about letting go of everything that isn't you -
all of the expectations, all of the beliefs – and
becoming who you are."

—Rachel Naomi Remen

CHAPTER
Twenty Four

Giving Back: Find A Higher Purpose

Have you noticed how people who are focused on a cause or a larger purpose in life have little time and energy for small irritations? Because they have a larger purpose, petty irritations seem of little or no consequence.

If you're a doctor or social worker fighting for the lives of patients or refugees in a war zone, small incidents will cease to affect you. Even running a business or having a busy career can take your focus off petty concerns.

Conversely, it is those who have little sense of purpose in their lives who fill their days sitting around watching soap operas and gossiping about others.

If you want to rise above petty everyday concerns, put your empathy, skills and energy to good use. Volunteer for a cause.

If you're single, you could travel to another country or region and help those affected by natural disasters or wars. If you have a family, you can still give back and contribute in your own community.

If you need some role models, read the stories or inspiring people who gave back. Visit www.naaree.com to read about the stories of Indian women achievers or read their biographies online.

Here are some websites where you can find organizations looking for volunteers in many fields.

volunteeringindia.com

ivolunteer.in

indicorps.org

ngosindia.com

ehsaas.org.in

sankalpindia.net

When you give back to others less fortunate than you, not only will you **shift your focus from judging the negative, to living the positive**, but you will live a more fulfilled life and feel good about yourself.

You'll also learn to see life from a larger perspective and your own problems will pale in comparison.

CHAPTER
Twenty Five

Oooh, You Diva, You!

You're awesome for completing this book and starting your transformation from Devi2Diva. Go to the link below to access the entire course with audio and videos online.

devi2diva.com/d2dprint

If you enjoyed this book do write a review on Amazon or share a testimonial with me at priyaflorence@gmail.com and let me know if I can use it on my course sign up page.

If you prefer, you can also record a video testimonial, upload it to YouTube and send me the link.

Here's some stuff to help you on your journey to greatness!

Free Master of My Fate Meditation Course

Sign up to download a Free Meditation at the link below

devi2diva.com/meditation

Listen to this empowering guided meditation daily and take back your power to become the master of your fate, captain of your soul.

Subscribe to the Naaree Talk Podcast

Subscribe to the Naaree Talk Podcast at the link below

naaree.com/podcast